THE BRITISH MUSEUM
BOOK OF EGYPTIAN
HIEROGLYPHS

COLOURED HIEROGLYPHS
FROM THE BRITISH MUSEUM

NEAL SPENCER

WITH ILLUSTRATIONS BY
CLAIRE THORNE

THE BRITISH MUSEUM PRESS

© The Trustees of The British Museum 2003

Published in 2003 by The British Museum Press
A division of The British Museum Company Ltd
46 Bloomsbury Street, London WC1B 3QQ

ISBN 0 7141 1957 1

Neal Spencer has asserted the right
to be identified as the author of this work.

A catalogue record for this title is available
from the British Library.

Designed and typeset by Harry Green.
Printed and bound in Hong Kong by C & C Offset

The hieroglyphs in the Introduction
and the Egyptian 'Alphabet' were drawn
by Richard Parkinson.

All photographs were taken by the Photography
and Imaging Dept of The British Museum,
© The Trustees of The British Museum,
except pages 7 and 11, © Redhead.

Jacket: Cartouche of Osiris lord of Abydos, from the
coffin of Amenemipet (pages 52-3). The background
hieroglyphs come from the base of the sarcophagus
of Ankhnesneferibre (page 73).

CONTENTS

INTRODUCTION

Crudely carved beneath a scene in the temple of Isis on Philae Island is the last known hieroglyphic inscription, dated to 394 AD. This date marks the end of nearly 3500 years of using the script to write the ancient Egyptian language. In the centuries following that last inscription, the ability to read hieroglyphs disappeared; during Medieval times, the signs were thought to represent mystical symbols. The modern breakthrough in understanding the language came in 1822, when the French scholar Jean-François Champollion made the assumption that the signs actually represented sounds. Using the trilingual inscription on the Rosetta Stone (fig. 1) in hieroglyphs, demotic and Greek, he first deciphered the name of Ptolemy V. Since then, the study of hieroglyphs has flourished, with thousands of texts translated. Egyptologists now avail themselves of multi-volume dictionaries and dozens of grammars of the language. Essentially, it is a script that can be studied like any other; a crucial difference is that we no longer know how it was pronounced. This is a result of the lack of written vowels, much like some modern languages such as Arabic. Nonetheless, the traditional language of Egypt's Christian population, Coptic, is a descendant of ancient Egyptian, and preserves some words from the language of the pharaonic civilization.

Egyptian hieroglyphs are images of humans, animals, geographical and plant forms (or parts thereof), alongside representations of man-made objects and more abstract signs. These depictions largely followed the conventions of Egyptian art: for example, the manner in which the human form was depicted in a combination of profile and front views. Three types of signs were employed to represent the ancient language: ideograms, phonograms and determinatives.

The simplest type of hieroglyphs are ideograms: single signs that conveyed a word. Thus the sign represents a simplified plan of a one-roomed building, and by extension the word *per*, or 'house'.

The principal group is the phonograms, or phonetic signs, which represent the individual sounds that form words. The basic ones represent twenty-four single consonants. For example, the sound *m* is denoted with the owl hieroglyph. These signs are the closest thing to the modern alphabet. This alphabet does not feature the same range of sounds as modern Western languages. In addition to the lack of vowels, there is no 'l', and guttural sounds are included, similar to those found in present-day Semitic languages. To read a text, Egyptologists transliterate the hieroglyphs into letters and diacritic signs, before then translating the words into English. In addition to single-consonant signs, a series of multi-consonantal signs were employed to represent

1 The Rosetta Stone, a royal decree carved on stone in three scripts: hieroglyphs, demotic and Greek. (196 BC, EA 24)

two or three consonants; about 150 signs of this type were used. A selection of the most common phonetic signs, alongside the transliteration and approximate sound value, are illustrated on pages 14-15.

The final type of sign is the determinative. These were placed at the end of a word, and indicated its meaning. This allowed a distinction to be made between words of different meaning but of a similar sound. The name 'Isis' is written with a determinative of a seated female ⟨glyph⟩. Another word with the same phonetic spelling is ⟨glyph⟩. The determinative is different, here being the same sign used as a ideogram for 'house'. This indicates that the word refers to a building, or part of one; in this case it is the word 'throne'. Some determinatives, such as human figures, are self-explanatory. Others are less clear ⟨glyph⟩: this sign represents a rolled up papyrus with seal, and was used to convey abstract notions such as memory or compassion. Through a knowledge of some basic signs, determinatives can help modern readers guess at the nature of a word without knowing its exact meaning.

With such a range in the types of sign, the person composing a text possessed a variety of possibilities for writing any word. For example, multi-consonant signs could be followed by a single-consonant hieroglyph that indicated the last sound value of the preceding sign, as if to help the reader. In the most shortened form of words, the determinative itself could represent the word alone, with no need for phonetic signs to be employed. A good example is the word for 'beer', *henqet*. One full writing is ⟨glyph⟩, where three phonetic signs precede a determinative representing a small beer jar. However, the word was most frequently written with the determinative alone ⟨glyph⟩; the nature of the text made it clear what the type of liquid was. Such abbreviations were particularly time-and labour-saving when carving a text into hard stone!

The number of signs is often staggering to the modern student of the language. Approximately 750 were used in the classic form of the script, Middle Egyptian. However, the majority are determinatives, frequently self-explanatory, such as the dozens of variants featuring a male figure. A knowledge of a few dozen phonetic signs and the basic group of determinatives would probably suffice for a basic ability to read the script. In much the same way, a limited vocabulary of signs can help modern viewers understand a reasonable amount of the texts upon statues and stelae. In sacred contexts, elaborate writings further complicated

2 Queen Hatshepsut being purified by the gods Horus and Thoth, from the temple of Amun at Karnak. (*c.* 1465 BC)

matters, and the temples of the Graeco-Roman period feature nearly 8,000 different signs in their inscriptions, many of which were complex mixtures of earlier signs. But these texts were not for reading by the average person: they were religious compositions seen by few and understood by fewer. Throughout Egyptian history, it is difficult to gauge how literate the population was, though 1% has been suggested. Ancient Egyptian texts were almost exclusively produced by or for the elite of society: royalty, wealthy government officials, scribes, priests and military men.

Those responsible for laying out texts would take great care in the spacing and arrangement of sign groups, to create a harmonious appearance. In effect, these groupings could also help the reader identify individual words with greater ease: spaces or punctuation were not used to denote gaps between words or the beginning of new phrases, sentences or paragraphs.

In addition to the variation afforded by the writing of individual words, texts could be orientated in three ways. The standard layout was right-to-left, as with modern Arabic, but other layouts are used: left-to-right, or top-to-bottom (but never bottom-to-top). It is easy to recognize in which direction the text should be read, as the animal and human signs face towards the front of the text. The orientation of a text was dictated by its context. For example, in temple scenes, the text would follow the orientation of the relevant figures of king or gods (fig. 2); symmetry was also coveted, as seen on many coffins and sarcophagi. Hieroglyphs are difficult to disassociate from art: scenes and texts were conceived as a whole, with one acting as a complement to the other. Only when text and representation are considered together can relief scenes or statuary be properly understood. For example, elaborate statues of kings could represent a writing of that pharaoh's name, through the sculpture's attributes and appearance.

Hieroglyphs were often written with exquisite detailing of individual signs, whether in paint or relief. This is particularly true of texts from sacred contexts: the decoration in the cult temples and tombs, and upon the statues and stelae found within. Such texts were intended to 'endure for eternity', and were addressed to both future generations and the gods. However, stylistic details were far from uniform: the form of signs and how texts were arranged changed through time, but also exhibit variations dependent on where the monument was produced, and the quality of the craftsmen and materials employed. Thus objects for the tomb, such as coffins and *Book of the Dead* papyri, could bear texts written in less formal hieroglyphs (see, for example, pages 48 and 59).

3 Ostracon bearing
a register of absences
from work, written in hieratic.
(*c.*1239 BC, EA 5634)

Soon after the appearance of hieroglyphs, a cursive script was developed to write the language, now known as hieratic. Such a development was inevitable, as hieroglyphs were rather cumbersome for writing mundane records of government administration or accounts. Hieratic was used for land contracts, wine-labels, inventories, some funerary texts, literary texts, trial records, love-letters, graffiti and census and absence lists (fig. 3).

From about 700 BC, another cursive script appeared, now known as demotic; this superseded hieratic. An example of its use is in the middle text upon the Rosetta Stone (see fig. 1). Demotic probably outlived hieroglyphs, as the latest demotic text dates to 452 AD, at Philae. Later still, Coptic, the script of Christian Egypt, was developed, borrowing signs from Greek. Hieratic and demotic were not generally used for texts upon temple walls, or carved on fine statuary: the standard medium was papyrus or ostraca (small flakes of limestone or fragments of pots, reused as ancient notepaper). Hieroglyphs persisted as the script for formal decoration of tombs and temples. The ancient Egyptians termed the script the 'divine speech'; the Greek word 'hieroglyphs' means 'sacred carvings'. Every hieroglyph in this book comes from an artefact which was originally intended for a temple or tomb.

This book concentrates almost exclusively on coloured hieroglyphs, a detail of immense importance to the ancient Egyptians. The colours used were principally based on mineral compounds, though organic matter such as charcoal was also employed. Each colour was imbued with a range of meanings, often contradictory, reflected in everything from statuary, paintings and amulets to architecture and hieroglyphic texts. Typically, the modern viewer can only grasp elements of ancient symbolism. Nonetheless, the colour green was evidently associated with rebirth and regeneration, explaining why the face of Osiris often bears this hue in paintings, relief and statuary. Yet he could also be shown with black skin, symbolizing his rulership over the Underworld. Within long and elaborate texts, each example of a sign was often written consistently with one colour, evidently believed to be a vital part of the hieroglyph. For example, in the finely painted and carved texts in the tomb of Seti I, the sun-disc hieroglyph was typically painted red (see pages 18-19). Complex hieroglyphs, of birds and gods, were often painted or inlaid with several colours. In relief scenes, the interaction between carved and painted detail is often apparent, alongside considerations of texture and material, and of course the architectural setting (fig. 4).

The examples in this book were chosen from amongst the extensive collections of the British

Museum, with two aims in mind. Firstly, the artwork highlights some of the variations of style and arrangement of hieroglyphs over 35 centuries of use, along with the striking use of colour. Each group of hieroglyphs is accompanied by a photograph of the object on which the text is found, thus hinting at the range of contexts in which coloured hieroglyphs were used. Secondly, the words and phrases chosen are amongst the most common seen upon statues, stelae and other monuments spread throughout the world's museums, but also upon the walls of the tombs and temples of Egypt. The artwork is not intended to be archaeological, merely faithful to the original. Thus where patches of paint have been lost, the colour has been restored in the drawing, to reflect its original appearance. This method allows the reader to appreciate the vigour and brightness of much ancient paintwork, particularly with those colour pigments vulnerable to degradation over time. Nonetheless, ancient details in the drawing and colouring of the signs are faithfully rendered, allowing the reader a glimpse at the vast range of styles deployed by Egyptian artists, from the carefully carved and painted reliefs in royal tombs, to the more spontaneous, fluent brushwork visible in small scale upon Third Intermediate Period coffins. Looked at in detail, some would not be out of place in a modern art museum.

4 Painted hieroglyphs and decoration in the Festival Hall of Tuthmosis III at Karnak. (c.1430 BC)

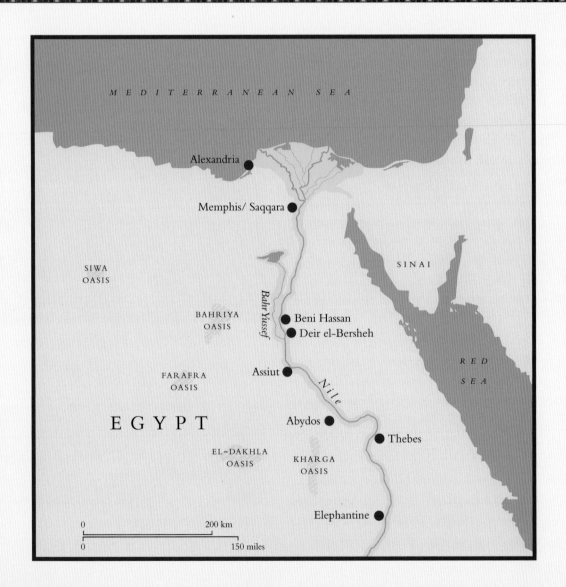

MEDITERRANEAN SEA

Alexandria

Memphis/ Saqqara

SIWA
OASIS

SINAI

BAHRIYA
OASIS

Bahr Yussef

Beni Hassan
Deir el–Bersheh

FARAFRA
OASIS

Assiut

Nile

RED
SEA

E G Y P T

Abydos

Thebes

EL–DAKHLA
OASIS

KHARGA
OASIS

Elephantine

0   200 km

0   150 miles

CHRONOLOGY OF ANCIENT EGYPT

Predynastic Period	c.4000–3100 BC
Early Dynastic Period	c.3100–2686 BC
Old Kingdom (Dynasties 4–6)	c.2686–2181 BC
First Intermediate Period	c.2181–2055 BC
Middle Kingdom (Dynasties 11–13)	c.2055–1650 BC
Second Intermediate Period	c.1650–1550 BC
New Kingdom (Dynasties 18–20)	c.1550–1069 BC
Third Intermediate Period	c.1069–664 BC
Late Period (Dynasties 26–30)	664–332 BC
Ptolemaic Period	305–30 BC
Roman Period	30 BC–AD 311

The signs are shown alongside
their approximate sound value.

SINGLE-CONSONANT SIGNS

	Sound value		Sound value		Sound value
	glottal stop		m		sh
	i		n		q
	y		r		k
	guttural sound		h		g
	w		h (emphatic)		t
	b		kh		tj
	p		khy		d
	f		s		dj

COMMON MULTI-CONSONANT SIGNS

	Sound value
	wen
	user
	per
	mi
	men
	mes
	neb
	nefer

	Sound value
	hat
	hem
	hes
	kheper
	sa
	sw
	di
	djed

NUMBERS

	1
	10
	100
	1000
	1,000,000
	½
	⅓

15

'KING OF UPPER AND LOWER EGYPT'

This title is that usually found before the king's *prenomen*, that is, the name given to him upon accession to the throne. The phrase is written with the sedge plant, symbolizing Upper Egypt (the Nile Valley south of Memphis), and the bee, representing Lower Egypt (the Delta). This small group of signs thus encapsulates one of the defining characteristics of ancient Egyptian kingship: that pharaoh was responsible for maintaining the union of two geographically distinct regions.

This text is part of the interior decoration of a coffin base. One of the scenes inside the coffin reflects another symbol of the duality inherent in Egyptian kingship. The coffin-owner, Amenemipet, is shown offering to two gods, Anubis and Ra-Horakhty. The former, seated to the left, wears the traditional double crown, which united the red crown of Lower Egypt with the white one of Upper Egypt.

Painted wooden coffin of the priest Amenemipet (detail)

Possibly from Thebes

Late 21st–early 22nd Dynasty (950–900 BC)

EA 22941

'SON OF RA'

Painted relief from the tomb of Seti I

From the Valley of the Kings, Thebes

19th dynasty, reign of Seti I (1294–1279 BC)

EA 5602

Pharaoh's *nomen*, or birth name, was typically preceded by this phrase, proclaiming the king's link to the creator sun-god. In *Papyrus Westcar*, a Middle Kingdom text set in the time of the Giza pyramids, one tale relates how three future kings would be fathered by Ra himself.

This section of relief from the tomb of Seti I reveals the high quality painted low-relief carving typical of royal tombs of the period. The attention to detail within some signs is striking, as evident in the hieroglyph of a goose. Though this is one of the most common signs, which represented the word 'son' or simply its phonetic value '*sa*', the sculptors and painters have carefully rendered the feathers in detail.

'HIS MAJESTY'

Both royal and private texts frequently feature this phrase; literally 'his servant' – as pharaoh was theoretically the High Priest of all the gods, and thus servant to the creator god.

As a whole, this scene depicts the arrival of tribute from Crete and two city-states in ancient Syria-Palestine, Hatta and Tunip. Each area is represented by distinct ethnic types, proffering praise, statues and vessels to pharaoh, who was depicted to the left of this scene. Tribute was exacted by pharaoh from vanquished enemies and vassal city-states, both on a regular basis and after military campaigns. Following the battle at Megiddo, Tuthmosis III claims to have returned with 340 prisoners, over 2,200 horses, nearly 900 enemy chariots, 200 bows and 24,000 livestock.

Tempera copy by Nina de Garis Davies (painted in 1930?), of a scene in the tomb of Menkheperresoneb at Thebes (TT 86).
18th dynasty, reign of Tuthmosis III (1479–1425 BC)
Department of Ancient Egypt and Sudan, archive.

Fragment of painted mud-plaster
from a private tomb
From Saqqara (?)
6th dynasty (2345–2181 BC)
EA 65927

Like the majority of Old Kingdom royal names, that of Pepi was written with simple phonetic signs alone. The *cartouche*, a stylized looped cord which surrounds the king's name, was reserved for royalty and occasionally gods.

This segment of painted text formed part of a list of estates which supplied the mortuary cult of a tomb-owner. Both royal and private funerary cults were supplied by domains scattered throughout Egypt. These agricultural lands were obliged to supply offerings for cult, theoretically for eternity. Many of these foundations were named after kings. This fragment refers to three estates, featuring the names of pharaohs Pepi I, Merenre and Neferkare (the throne name of Pepi II).

'KING OF UPPER AND LOWER EGYPT KHEPERKARA,

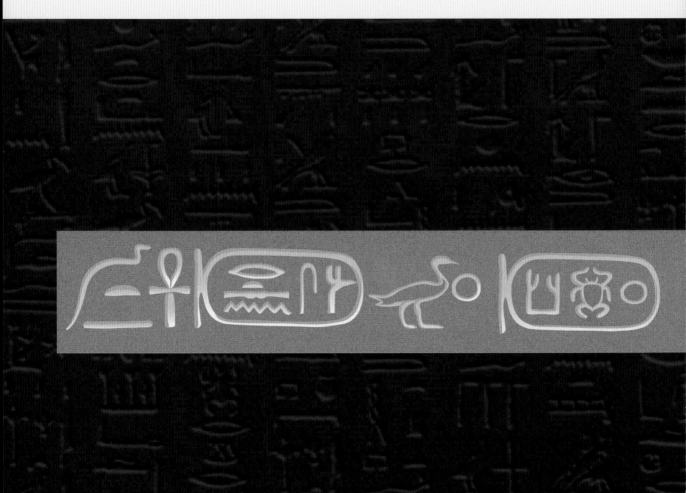

The two most important of the five royal names taken on by pharaohs are carved upon this private stela. Senwosret, the first in a line of three kings with this name, took the throne name Kheperkara upon accession as pharaoh. In a trait familiar from many names containing a divine element, the name of the god Ra is written first within the cartouche (as one reads right to left), despite it being the last element pronounced.

Limestone stela of Intef

From Abydos

12th dynasty, reign of Senwosret I (1965–1920 BC)

EA 562

The remainder of the text upon Intef's red-painted stela describes an idealized portrait of the man ('I gave bread to the hungry, beer to the thirsty'), who claims he was appointed as overseer of the palace by Senwosret I. Intef is depicted leaning upon a staff, at the lower left of the stela.

'AHMOSE-NEFERTARI'

Fragment of painted wall-plaster
from the tomb of Kynebu
Thebes
20th dynasty, reign of Ramses VIII
(1129–1126 BC)
EA 37994

Ahmose-Nefertari was the longest-remembered queen in ancient Egypt, at least according to the preserved record. She was the wife of Ahmose, the king responsible for ousting the Hyksos (who had occupied parts of Egypt for over a century) and mother to his successor Amenhotep I.

The painting comes from the tomb of a priest who lived nearly four hundred years after Ahmose-Nefertari. During the Ramesside period, the queen became revered as a saint, particularly by the workmen responsible for building and decorating the royal tombs in the Valley of the Kings. People would recite prayers and donate offerings, and seek advice on matters spiritual or mundane, from statues of the long-deceased queen and her son Amenhotep I.

'MENKHEPERRA' (TUTHMOSIS III)

Tuthmosis III's throne name, Menkheperra, is one of the most commonly encountered names upon the objects surviving from ancient Egypt. In addition to many statues and temple decorations, the name is very frequently carved on scarabs, even those produced long after the death of the pharaoh (1479–1425 BC). Evidently his name was thought to bring good fortune.

This king list was set up by Ramses II in his temple at Abydos, to create a link with a long line of royal ancestors. Such lists have proved enormously useful for modern scholars, in reconstructing the order of kings. However, there are difficulties, as kings who ruled in parallel, for instance over different areas of the country, would still be listed consecutively. More crucially, certain rulers were omitted entirely, as these were not thought to embody the ideals of pharaonic kingship. On this list, none of the pharaohs connected with the Amarna heresy, including Akhenaten and Tutankhamun, are featured.

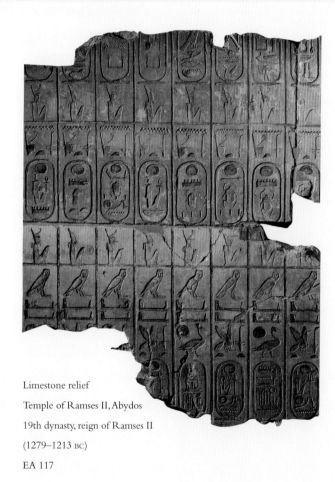

Limestone relief
Temple of Ramses II, Abydos
19th dynasty, reign of Ramses II
(1279–1213 BC)
EA 117

Nebmaatre was the throne name of Amenhotep III (1390–1352 BC), who presided over a period in which Egypt prospered through a time of little conflict, leading to artistic innovation and a wide-ranging construction programme.

At his mortuary temple on the west bank at Thebes, the king set up hundreds of large statues of gods and goddesses, particularly the lioness-deity Sekhmet. In addition, the temple was provided with a series of colossal figures of the king, including the celebrated *Colossi of Memnon*, which still stand over 18 m (59 ft) tall. Towards the end of his reign, he celebrated three jubilee festivals, proclaiming his rebirth as the sun-god.

Detail from the king-list (see page 29)

Temple of Ramses II, Abydos

19th dynasty, reign of Ramses II (1279–1213 BC)

EA 117

Limestone statue of Amenhotep III

Mortuary temple of Amenhotep III, Thebes

18th dynasty, reign of Amenhotep III (1390–1352 BC)

EA 3

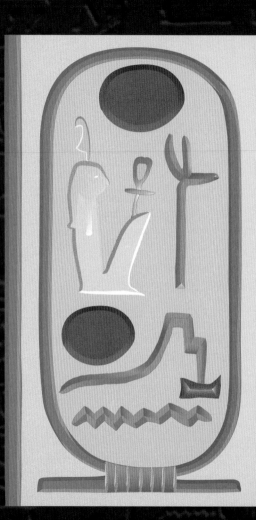

Usermaatra-setepenra, the throne name of Ramses II (1279–1213 BC), is undoubtedly the cartouche most frequently visible on ancient Egyptian monuments. On this statue (*right*), it is carved on the king's right shoulder. In addition to the temples, statues and obelisks commissioned by Ramses II throughout Egypt, he added his name to hundreds of existing monuments; an efficient method of ensuring one's legacy towards the gods.

During his 66-year reign, Ramses II founded a new capital in the north-east of Egypt, called Per-Ramses ('the house of Ramses'). Ramses led a series of military campaigns in Nubia, Canaan, Phoenicia and Syria, and built a line of forts along the western edge of the Delta. He is known to have fathered at least 96 children; three of his sons were elected successors to the throne but died before their long-lived father.

Detail from the king-list (see page 29)

Temple of Ramses II, Abydos

19th dynasty, reign of Ramses II (1279–1213 BC)

EA 117

Granite statue of Ramses II

Temple of Khnum, Elephantine

19th dynasty, reign of Ramses II (1279–1213 BC)

EA 67

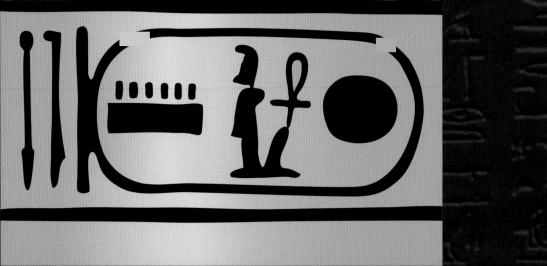

'MENMAATRA' (SETI I)

The throne name of Seti I is Menmaatra, again written with the disc of the sun-god given the prominent first place. After the cartouche, two signs make up the phrase 'true of voice', an epithet applied to the blessed deceased, both royal and non-royal.

These hieroglyphs come from the first line of the text carved upon a shabti, or funerary statuette, of Seti I. These small figures were placed in tombs as substitutes to perform any agricultural labour required of the deceased in the afterlife. In later times, burials were provided with sets of 401 shabtis: one for each day of the year, and a foreman for each group of ten. Royal burials of the New Kingdom, such as that of Tutankhamun, were endowed with shabtis produced in a stunning variety of materials, from gilded wood to examples in highly glazed blue faience.

Glazed composition shabti of Seti I
Thebes, Valley of the Kings, tomb of Seti I
19th dynasty, reign of Seti I (1294–1279 BC)
EA 22818

TITLE

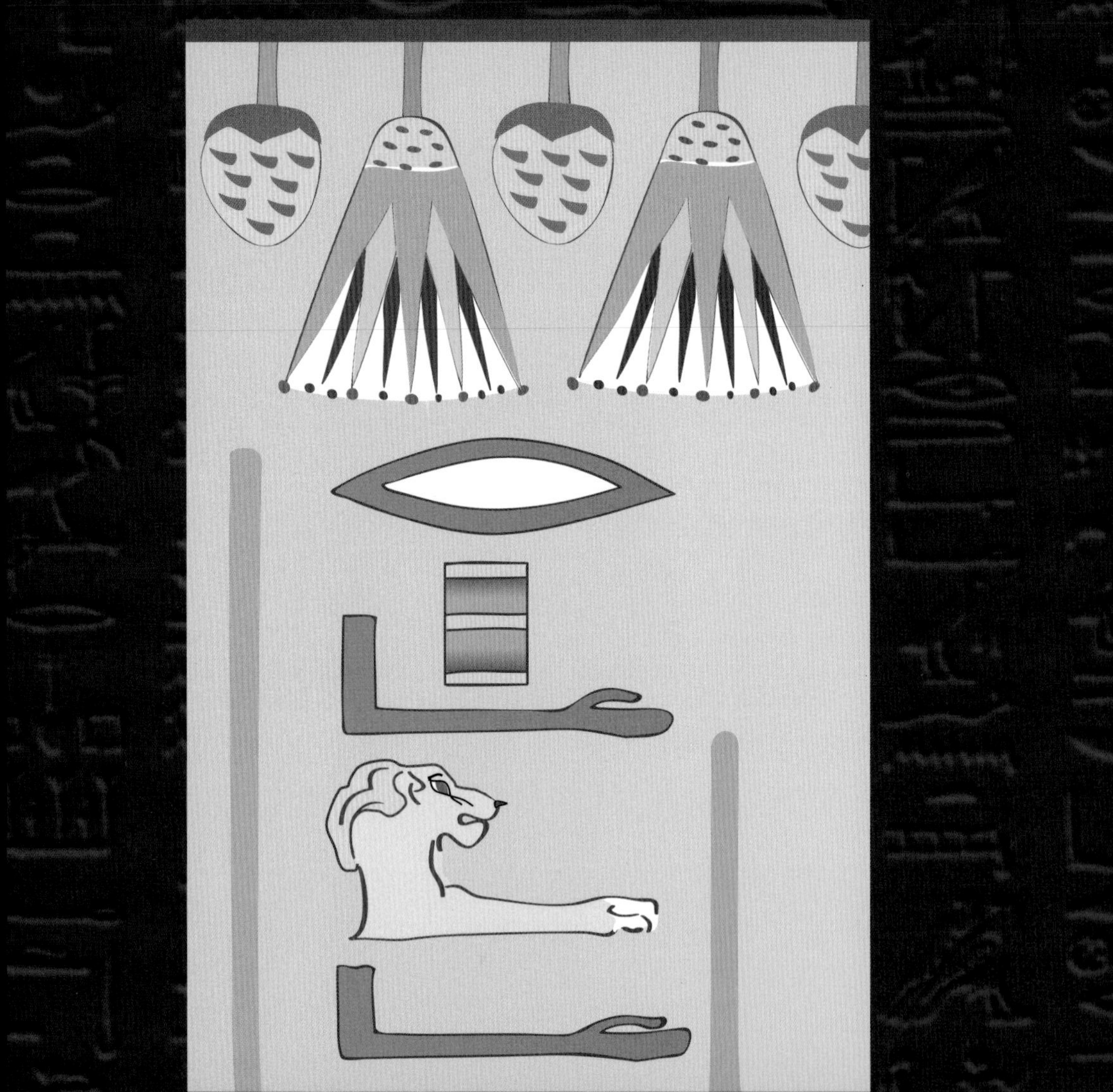

'HEREDITARY PRINCE, MAYOR'

Originally, these titles referred to the crown prince and the supreme civil official at regional towns throughout Egypt. However, the phrases soon became honorific. By the Late Period, nearly all officials preceded their actual occupations with these titles – the phrase had merely come to mean 'important official'.

In this scene, from the tomb of the chief steward Kenamun, the young pharaoh Amenhotep II is shown on the lap of his mother. Nine captives are crouched beneath the king's feet and restrained on a rope held in his hands. This detail symbolized pharaoh's control over the 'Nine Bows', the peoples of Egypt and its adjacent lands.

Tempera copy by Nina de Garis Davies (between 1911 and 1928), of a scene in the tomb of Kenamun at Thebes (TT 93)
18th dynasty, reign of Amenhotep II (1427–1400 BC)
Department of Ancient Egypt and Sudan, archive.

'Sealbearer of Lower Egypt' is one of the titles most commonly found on private monuments. By the middle of the Old Kingdom, the title was not relevant to the duties of the person; it forms one of a string of titles that were merely honorific. Such titles aimed to imply a close association with pharaoh.

Wahibre was an overseer of frontiers and a general. This over-lifesize statue was undoubtedly dedicated in a temple, possibly to Osiris, who is depicted in the small shrine held upon the official's knees. Through setting up such statues, officials hoped to prompt priests and visitors to the temple into reciting an offering prayer on their behalf.

Basalt statue of Wahibre
Provenance unknown
26th Dynasty (664–525 BC)
EA 111

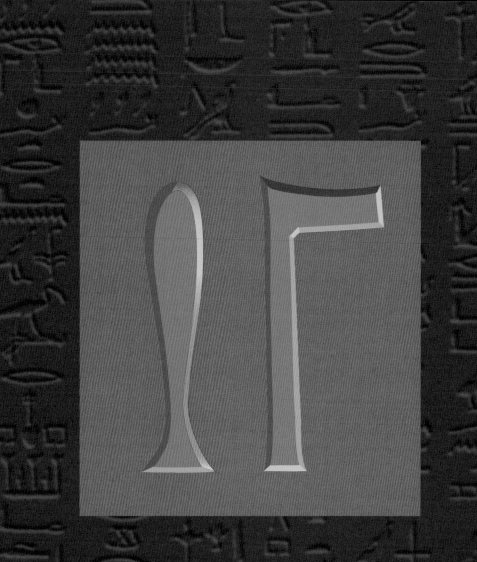

'PRIEST'

The priesthoods of ancient Egyptian temples were arranged into strict hierarchies, headed by the High Priest. One of the basic positions was that of 'servant of the god'; the same person could hold titles in several priesthoods relating to different cults.

Ptahshepses was a prominent official who lived during the pyramid age, serving as an official under Menkaure (builder of the third pyramid at Giza), and six subsequent pharaohs. His close relationship with the throne was underlined by his marriage to a royal daughter, Khaimaat. This false door would have been the focal point of the tomb chapel of the deceased. Through this architectural medium, magical sustenance would be transferred to the body, buried in a chamber beneath the chapel.

Limestone false-door of Ptahshepses

Saqqara

5th dynasty, reign of Niuserre (?) (c.2416–2392 BC)

EA 682

'LECTOR PRIEST'

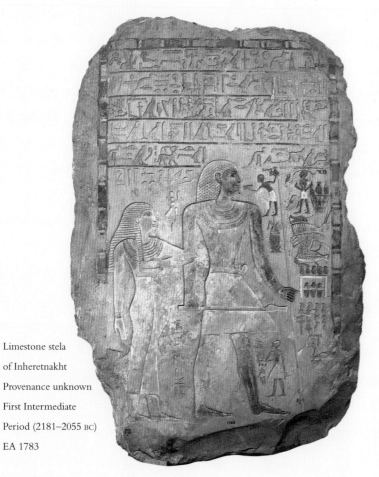

Limestone stela
of Inheretnakht
Provenance unknown
First Intermediate
Period (2181–2055 BC)
EA 1783

The lector-priest was in a position to oversee certain rituals in the daily temple cult, but also played a central role in the mortuary cult. Inheretnakht, who commissioned this stela, was also 'a mayor, sealbearer and sole companion'. He is depicted wearing a kilt, collar and wig, while holding staff and sceptre; common attire for elite men depicted on funerary monuments.

The text comprises a standardized offering prayer and formulaic praises of the deceased's worthy actions in life. Stylistic details, such as the lack of a baseline beneath the figures' feet, their bodily proportions and the narrow space afforded to the offerings, are typical of many First Intermediate Period stelae. At this period, Egypt had fragmented into a series of political units, resulting in different artistic styles developing where no access to court artists was possible.

In a society where the written record was so central to elite culture, yet the levels of literacy were low, scribes were held in high esteem. It was they who wrote the religious texts held in temple libraries, inked a copy of a *Book of the Dead*, or laid out a legal contract. As such, it is unsurprising to find scribes linked to all areas of Egyptian life, from the royal court and government administration, to the temples and military.

Djedhoriuefankh would have been one of many scribes attached to the great temple at Karnak, evidently with particular responsibility for tracking the movement of the produce used in the daily offering cult. Through this position he could avail himself of a richly decorated coffin. In this scene from the decoration of the base, Djedhoriuefankh is shown offering to the sun-god Ra-Horakhty and one of the four sons of Horus, Imsety.

Painted wooden coffin of Djedhoriuefankh (detail)

From Thebes

21st dynasty (1069–945 BC)

EA 22900

'GENERAL'

It is unclear how much of a permanent army existed in the Middle Kingdom, though provincial rulers clearly had the ability to marshall significant force when needed. Sepi was buried in a shaft tomb, cut into the forecourt of the tomb chapel of Djehutyhotep, the principal official of the Beni Hassan region. Therefore, Sepi must have been part of Djehutyhotep's immediate entourage.

Rectangular wood coffins, decorated with blue hieroglyphs spelling out an offering text and the owner's name and titles, are typical of elite burials of the Middle Kingdom. A pair of *udjat*-eyes allowed the deceased to 'see' the rising sun to the East, while the false-door depicted below ensured offerings were transmitted to the body for eternity.

Cedar coffin of Sepi
From Deir el-Bersha
Mid- to late 12th dynasty
(*c.*1900–1795 BC)
EA 55315

'AMUN-RA KING OF GODS'

Amun, or 'hidden one', became a prominent god in the 11th dynasty. He would remain the most important god at Thebes until the end of pharaonic civilization. However, he is most frequently encountered when united with the sun-god Ra, to form the creator- and sun-god Amun-Ra, often qualified as 'king of gods'. Amun-Ra was worshipped in the massive temple complex at Karnak, as well as at sites throughout Egypt.

The base of this coffin was decorated with a scene of king Amenhotep I, who lived five centuries before the coffin owner Djedhoriuefankh. This reflects the high esteem in which this king was held by the inhabitants of Thebes. The name 'Amenhotep' signifies 'Amun is content': many pharaohs and private individuals of the New Kingdom and Third Intermediate Period had names referring to this god.

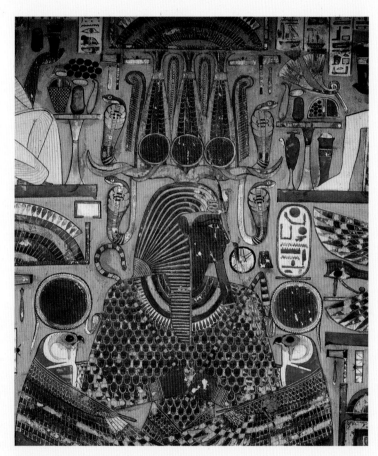

Painted wooden coffin of Djedhoriuefankh (detail)

From Thebes

21st dynasty (1069–945 BC)

EA 22900

'RA'

Ra, the embodiment of the sun (his name is written with the sun-disc and divine determinative) is known from the Early Dynastic period. His importance as creator-god was unparalleled in the Old Kingdom, when the pyramid-building kings often featured the god's name as part of their own. His principal cult centre was Heliopolis, literally 'city of the sun' in Greek.

This writing of his name comes from the *Book of Gates* depicted in Seti I's tomb. The composition describes the nocturnal journey of the sun-god through the underworld in a barque. During this voyage, he had to navigate through the dangers of the 12 hours of the night. The provision of such compositions in royal tombs ensured the king would be successfully reborn every morning.

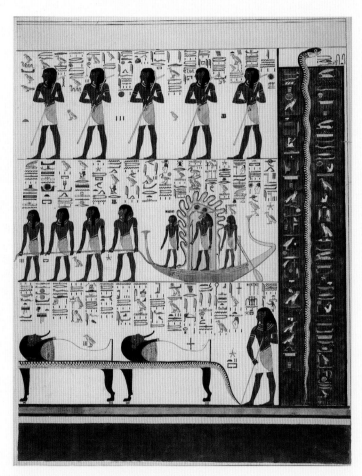

Water-colour by Henry Salt (1780–1827) of a scene from the *Book of Gates* depicted in the tomb of Seti I
19th dynasty, reign of Seti I (1294–1279 BC)
Department of Ancient Egypt and Sudan, archive

Osiris was the lord of the afterlife, with whom the deceased was identified after death. Here, his name is written in the cartouche usually reserved for pharaohs. Within the cartouche, Osiris is given the epithet 'lord of Abydos', a reference to the god's historic cult centre 75 km (46 miles) north of Thebes.

The detail comes from the base of an anthropoid wooden coffin, decorated with a series of small, highly-coloured scenes depicting the gods of the Underworld. Such decoration is typical on elite coffins of the Third Intermediate Period. In a period when tomb decoration was almost non-existent, these scenes would help ensure the safe passage of the deceased through the Underworld.

Painted wooden coffin of the priest
Amenemipet
From Thebes (?)
Late 21st–early 22nd Dynasty (950–900 BC)
EA 22941

'ANUBIS'

Glazed composition funerary pectoral
Provenance unknown
19th dynasty (1295–1186 BC)
EA 29370

Anubis was primarily one of the gods of the afterlife. He attended to the mummified body before burial, and featured in the Judgement Scene in the *Book of the Dead*. He is typically depicted as a recumbent jackal, as on this pectoral, or as a jackal-headed man. Here, the hieroglyphic label uses the latter form as a determinative.

The shape of this pectoral echoes the monumental pylons that fronted Egyptian temples of the New Kingdom and later. It would have been placed on the chest of the mummified body; the presence of Anubis ensured protection for the body.

'HATHOR CHIEF ONE OF THE WEST'

Hathor was a goddess typically depicted as a cow, and was associated with love, childbirth, music and festival. In this relief, she is depicted as a female figure, though the cow-horns allude to her typical appearance. The tiny hieroglyphs upon her dress include the wish that Seti I enjoys 'millions of years and hundreds of thousands of festivals'.

In the royal tombs in the Valley of the Kings, Hathor acts as a guarantee of a successful afterlife and the rejuvenator of the deceased. Here she offers a ritual collar to Seti I. Hathor takes on the guise of 'the goddess of the West' in many royal tombs, and is qualified as such in this text. The West is where the sun sets every day, and by extension, the realm of the dead. The cemeteries at Thebes were located on the west bank of the Nile.

Water-colour by Henry Salt (1780–1827), of a scene from the tomb of Seti I. 19th dynasty, reign of Seti I (1294–1279 BC) Department of Ancient Egypt and Sudan, archive.

The throne sign ⌐ was used to write the name Isis, usually followed by a divine determinative. However, art and hieroglyphs were often conceived in a unified fashion: this example shows how the relevant sign is used to distinguish Isis from other female goddesses. In this vignette, she embraces Osiris, the god of the afterlife, within a shrine topped by uraei (royal cobras).

This detail is from one of the painted vignettes that accompany the spells in the *Book of the Dead* of Ani. Ani was a royal scribe, accounting scribe of the offerings of all the gods, and overseer of granaries associated with the gods of Abydos. This papyrus provided Ani with the necessary spells to overcome the perils of the afterlife. Spell 125A, which accompanies this scene, contains the necessary statements to allow entry into the Hall of Two Truths, and a short hymn to Osiris.

Papyrus sheet from the *Book of the Dead* of Ani

From Thebes

19th dynasty, 1295–1186 BC

EA 10470/30

'AN OFFERING
THAT THE KING GIVES'

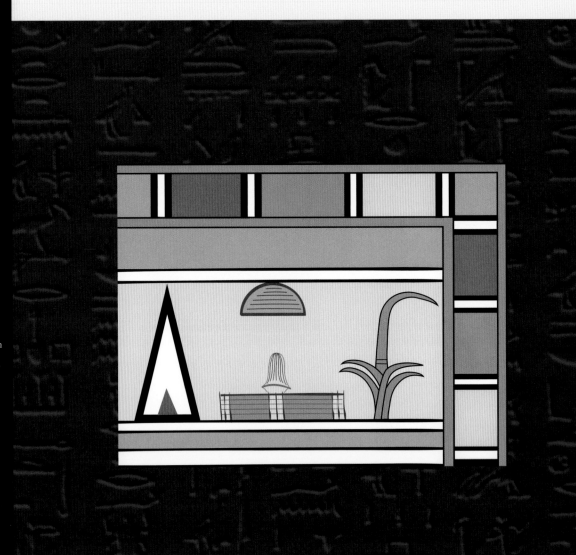

Painted wooden
coffin of Sen
(detail)
Deir el-Bersha
12th dynasty
(1985–1795 BC)
EA 30841

THE OFFERING FORMULA

The offering formula appears in the late First Intermediate Period, and is one of the most common types of texts preserved on ancient Egyptian monuments. It is typically found on stelae erected in tomb-chapels, but abbreviated versions were also inscribed on coffins and on statues set up in temples. Essentially, it was a funerary prayer which would invoke a series of material offerings for the deceased. The opening phrase reflected the ideology that all officials were reliant on the king. The stela of Senwosret (*right*) provides an example of a classic offering formula, above a scene of husband and wife before an offering table:

'An offering that the king gives to Osiris lord of Busiris, great god of Abydos. May he give offerings of bread, beer, oxen and fowl, linen and alabaster, and every good and pure thing on which a god lives, for the *ka* of the honoured one before Osiris, Senwosret, true of voice.'

Painted limestone stela of Senwosret

Provenance unknown

12th dynasty (1985–1795 BC)

EA 198

'A THOUSAND OF BREAD AND BEER; A THOUSAND OF OXEN AND FOWL; A THOUSAND OF LINEN AND ALABASTER; A THOUSAND OF INCENSE AND OIL'

The offering table is piled with copious amounts of bread, fruit, meat, vegetables, and garlands of flowers. Vessels of precious metals are depicted above. These offerings provided a substitute for eternal sustenance if the mortuary cult was neglected. The elaborate painted hieroglyphs provided further insurance that food offerings were guaranteed for perpetuity.

The decoration in the tomb-chapel of Nebamun represents one of the finest expressions of Egyptian painting. Though the location of the tomb is now unknown, eleven segments of the wall-paintings survive in the British Museum. The style of the painting places Nebamun in the later part of the 18th dynasty, when he held the title of inspector of grains.

Painted plaster scene from the tomb of Nebamun
From Thebes
18th dynasty, reign of Tuthmosis IV or Amenhotep III (1400–1352 BC)
EA 37985

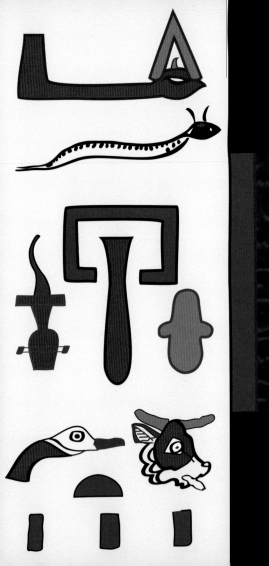

'HE GIVES OFFERINGS OF BREAD, BEER, OXEN AND FOWL'

This central phrase in the offering formula introduced the list of offerings which the deceased would hope to receive as part of the mortuary cult. The four basic components (bread, beer, oxen and fowl) are written in abbreviated form: these products are present in nearly every offering formula. While bread and beer reflected the basic diet of all ancient Egyptians, oxen and fowl were probably less widely available.

Tanetaa, the woman buried in this coffin, was married to Pasenhor, who belonged to the Meshwesh tribe, a group of peoples from Libya that settled in Egypt from the late New Kingdom onwards. The style and quality of both Tanetaa and Pasnehor's coffins reveal how Egyptianized the Meshwesh had become, rising to positions of prominence within Egyptian society.

Side panel from the wooden coffin of Tanetaa

From Thebes

25th dynasty (747–625 BC)

EA 30360

'EVERY GOOD AND PURE THING'

This phrase often finishes the offering formula that precedes the deceased's name, usually as part of the statement 'every good and pure thing on which a god lives'. Through such a generalized statement, the formula was effectively encompassing all manner of offering goods which could not be mentioned in the limited space available.

This coffin also dates to the 25th or 26th dynasty, and provides a nice example of how the basic offering formula, first developed in the late First Intermediate Period, persisted for more than a millennium. In this example, six different gods are invoked by the offering formulae: Ptah–Sokar–Osiris, Anubis, Hathor, Ra–Horakhty, Atum and Osiris lord of Abydos.

Base of the inner wooden coffin of
Tjatjenef
From Beni Hassan
25th–26th dynasty (747–525 BC)
EA 32052

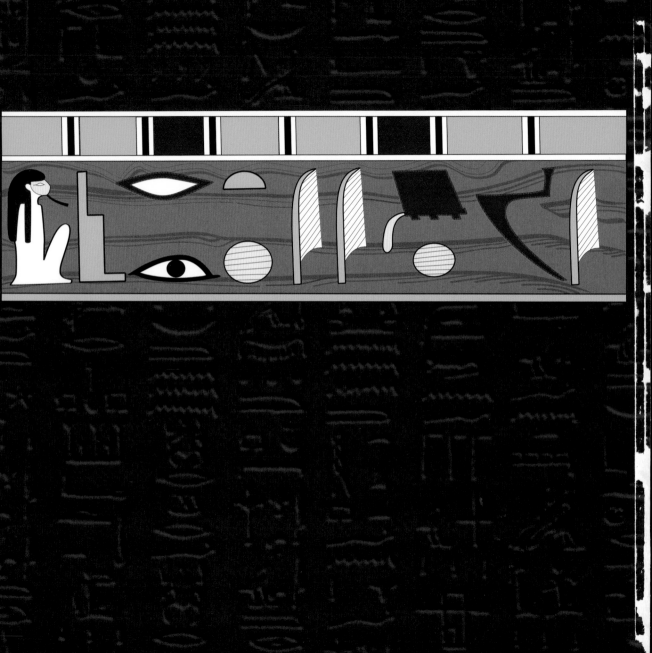

'HONOURED BEFORE OSIRIS'

This epithet was conferred upon the dead, and implies they were accepted in the afterlife by the god Osiris. After the Old Kingdom, the deceased was identified with Osiris. In the offering formulae found on stelae and coffins, this phrase usually precedes the titles and name of the owner.

The fine multi-coloured hieroglyphs, painted onto wood, are a typical feature on rectangular coffins of the Middle Kingdom. These were commissioned for the burials of elite families at regional towns such as Assiut, 200 km (124 miles) north of Thebes.

End-board from the wooden coffin of Intef

From Assiut

12th dynasty (1985–1795 BC)

EA 46644

'DONATING WINE'

Bread and beer were the fundamental parts of the daily offering rituals that would occur within the sanctuaries of the god's temples. However, a variety of other goods were also presented to the divine image, including incense, milk, meat and wine. Temple estates often owned vineyards throughout Egypt: wine would be transported from areas such as the oases and Delta, in large ceramic amphorae bearing labels.

This finely-painted relief was found amongst others in the ruins of one of the temples at Deir el-Bahri. An offering table is shown laden with meat, bread and grapes. The original scene depicted a standing king offering two wine jars to a god; the edge of pharaoh's kilt and a hand holding a jar can be seen at the right side of the relief.

Painted limestone temple relief
Thebes, Deir el-Bahri
18th dynasty, reign of Hatshepsut
or Tuthmosis III (1479–1425 BC)
EA 782

OTHER COMMON PHRASES AND WORDS

'LIFE, STABILITY, DOMINION'

Black siltstone sarcophagus
of Ankhnesneferibre
Thebes, Deir el-Medina
26th dynasty, reign of Amasis
(570–526 BC)
EA 32

These three signs are typically found on royal funerary monuments, and represent three central aspects to the afterlife sought by royal persons. Eternal life could be granted to humans by the gods. Stability reflected the Egyptian desire for an existence unaffected by the forces of chaos. Finally, dominion proclaimed divine-like authority over subjects.

This monumental sarcophagus was found in a narrow shaft tomb cut into the cliff face behind the abandoned workman's village of Deir el-Medina, where it had been re-used by a Ptolemaic priest. Its original owner, depicted on the lid, was Ankhnesneferibre, daughter of pharaoh Psamtek II. As God's Wife of Amun, she played an important political and religious role at Thebes, during an era when pharaoh resided in the north of Egypt.

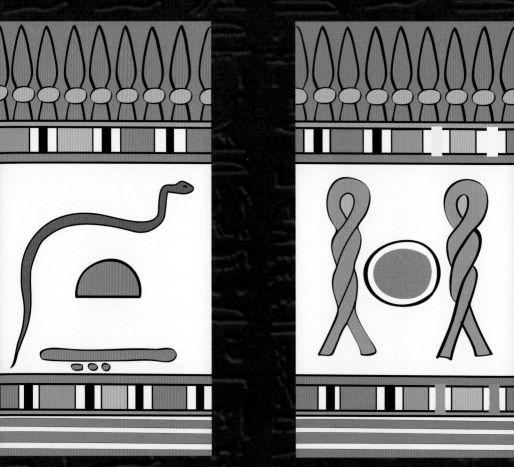

'ETERNITY'

Egyptian texts use two words to describe eternity, *djet* and *neheh*. The exact nature of the distinction between the two types is unclear. In certain texts, *djet* conjures up associations with Osiris and the earth, whereas *neheh* alludes to the solar cycle, and thus the sun-god Ra. Nonetheless, the two types of eternity are often invoked together: a common phrase is the wish to 'live for *djet* and *neheh*', thus encompassing all possible manner of time.

Painted wooden coffin of Hor
From Thebes
22nd dynasty (945–715 BC)
EA 6659

This is the essence of Egyptian beliefs regarding the afterlife: the pious individual, if benefiting from a good burial and the necessary mortuary cult, would exist forever, enjoying similar experiences to those in their earthly life. The mummy found inside this coffin revealed the owner died in middle age.

'HIS SON'

Funerary monuments, including stelae, statuary and tomb decoration, often featured the family of the deceased. Here, Nebamun is shown with wife and daughter, fowling in the marshes. However, in ancient Egypt, it was the son who was held in particularly high esteem, being responsible for a proper burial of his father, and also fulfilling the role of mortuary priest (who ensured offerings were supplied to sustain the deceased).

In reality, the mortuary cult was often undertaken by someone other than the son, particularly if, before death, an endowment had been arranged for a priest to carry out ritual and offerings at the tomb. Such arrangements were supposed to last for eternity. Few lasted more than a generation, though certain persons received posthumous cult for centuries.

Painted plaster scene from the tomb of Nebamun

From Thebes

18th dynasty, reign of Tuthmosis IV or Amenhotep III (1400–1352 BC)

EA 37977 (the hieroglyphs for 'his son' are from another fragment of this tomb's decoration, EA 37985, pictured on page 63)

'HIS WIFE'

Husband and wife were frequently
buried in the same tomb. However,
the male typically retained a prominent
position in the decoration upon funerary
monuments. This is evident upon this
stela, as Hedjeret, wife of the scribe
Samontu, is depicted at a smaller scale,
standing behind her husband. The couple
sit before a table laden with offerings,
while their children are depicted in the
register below. Samontu held a series
of scribal positions, to which he was
appointed by King Amenemhat III.

There is no evidence for a marriage
ceremony in ancient Egypt, though many
legal texts outline details of inheritance
through marriage and even lengthy
divorce proceedings. Women did not
hold the same legal privileges as men:
at divorce, they could claim only one
third of the common property of the
married couple. Nonetheless, women
could own land and hire labour.

Limestone stela of Samontu

Provenance unknown

12th dynasty, reign of

Amenemhat II (1922–1878 BC)

EA 828

FURTHER READING

FOR BEGINNERS

Parkinson, R.B. *The British Museum Pocket Guide to Ancient Egyptian Hieroglyphs.* London, British Museum Press 2003.

Collier, M. & Manley, B. *How to Read Egyptian Hieroglyphs.* London, British Museum Press 1998.

GRAMMARS AND DICTIONARIES

Allen, J. *Middle Egyptian.* Cambridge University Press, 2000.

Faulkner, R. O., *A Concise Dictionary of Middle Egyptian.* Griffith Institute, Oxford 1962.

Gardiner, A. H., *Egyptian Grammar: Being an Introduction to the Study of Hieroglyphs* (3rd ed.). Oxford University Press, Oxford 1957.

ANTHOLOGIES OF TRANSLATIONS

Lichtheim, M., *Ancient Egyptian Literature: A Book of Readings* (3 vols). University of California Press, Berkeley, 1973–1980.

Parkinson, R. B., *Voices from Ancient Egypt: An Anthology of Middle Kingdom Writings.* British Museum Press, London 1991.

McDowell, A., *Village Life in Ancient Egypt: Laundry Lists and Love Songs.* Oxford University Press, Oxford 2001.

CONTEXT: ART, HISTORY AND CULTURE

Baines, J. and Málek, J., *Cultural Atlas of Ancient Egypt.* Phaidon, Oxford 1980; revised ed. Checkmark Books, New York.

Davies, W.V. (ed.). *Colour and Painting in ancient Egypt.* London, British Museum Press 2001.

Davies, W.V. & Friedman, R.F. *Egypt.* London, British Museum Press 1998.

Faulkner, R. O. *The Ancient Egyptian Book of the Dead* (revised ed. C. A. R. Andrews). British Museum Publications, London 1985.

Parkinson, R.B. *Cracking Codes. The Rosetta Stone & decipherment.* London, British Museum Press 1999.

Smith, W. S., *The Art and Architecture of Ancient Egypt* (revised ed. W. K. Simpson). Pelican History of Art; Yale University Press, New Haven and London 1998.

Taylor, J.T. *Death & the Afterlife in Ancient Egypt.* London, British Museum Press 2001.

Wilkinson, R.H. *Reading Egyptian art: hieroglyphic guide to ancient Egyptian painting and sculpture.* London, Thames & Hudson 1992.

For bibliography on other aspects of ancient Egypt, contact the Department of Ancient Egypt and Sudan at The British Museum, Great Russell Street, London WC1B 3DG or visit www.thebritishmuseum.ac.uk/egyptian

For information on other British Museum Press books, contact the Marketing Assistant at British Museum Press, 46 Bloomsbury Street, London WC1B 3QQ

Email: sales.books@bmcompany.co.uk or visit www.britishmuseum.co.uk